UNDERCOVER STORY

THE HIDDEN STORY OF
HOMELESSNESS

Karen Latchana Kenney

raintree

a Capstone company — publishers for children

Raintree is an imprint of Capstone Global Library Limited, a company incorporated in England and Wales having its registered office at 264 Banbury Road, Oxford OX2 7DY – Registered company number: 6695582

www.raintree.co.uk
myorders@raintree.co.uk

Text © Capstone Global Library Limited 2016
The moral rights of the proprietor have been asserted.

Produced for Raintree by Calcium
Edited by Sarah Eason and Jen Sanderson
Designed by Keith Williams
Picture research by Sarah Eason
Production by Victoria Fitzgerald
Originated by Capstone Global Library Ltd © 2016
Printed and bound in China

ISBN 978 1 4747 1639 0
19 18 17 16 15
10 9 8 7 6 5 4 3 2 1

British Library Cataloguing in Publication Data
A full catalogue record for this book is available from the British Library

Acknowledgements
We would like to thank the following for permission to reproduce photographs: Dreamstime: Alexraths 37, Amaviael 29, Americanspirit 33, 43, Annworthy 34, Anthonyata 27, Designpicssub 38, Hurricanehank 31, Landd09 30, Leaf 23, Lisafx 40, Outline205 24, Wardrip Design 44, Wrangler 39; Shutterstock: Alexander Image 17, Robert J. Daveant 13, DJTaylor 18, Brian Eichhorn 9, Ejwhite 16, Glovatskiy 8, Chris Harvey 22, I4Icocl2 6, Monkey Business Images 7, 15, 20, Ildi Papp 14, Julia Pivovarova 28, Ronfromyork 10, Serge Bertasius Photography 36, Richard Thornton 4, Wrangler 1, 5, 12.

Cover photographs reproduced with permission of: iStockphoto: Blue Cutler.

Every effort has been made to contact copyright holders of material reproduced in this book. Any omissions will be rectified in subsequent printings if notice is given to the publisher.

All the internet addresses (URLs) given in this book were valid at the time of going to press. However, due to the dynamic nature of the internet, some addresses may have changed, or sites may have changed or ceased to exist since publication. While the author and publisher regret any inconvenience this may cause readers, no responsibility for any such changes can be accepted by either the author or the publisher.

Some words are shown in bold, **like this**. You can find out what they mean by looking in the glossary.

CONTENTS

THE TRUTH ABOUT HOMELESSNESS

In cities and towns around the world, people experience homelessness every day. Many see homeless people on the streets, but walk past the homeless as if they are invisible. Homelessness is a problem people have become used to seeing. However, it is one that is not going away and it affects thousands of people each year.

Homelessness is simply not having a home. Someone might stay under a bridge or in a tent for shelter, but not every homeless person lives on the streets or "sleeps rough". A homeless person can find shelter in the homes of friends or relatives. However, that shelter is not permanent and staying there is a temporary solution. It is still homelessness.

ANYONE CAN BE HOMELESS

All ages and types of person can become homeless. It can happen to almost anyone. Homelessness has many causes. Sometimes, the loss of a job causes a family to become homeless. One pay cheque can mean the difference between having and not having a home.

Many people become homeless when the economy is bad.

Sometimes, **domestic violence** is the cause of homelessness. Women and their children may leave the family home to escape violence, and become homeless as a result. Mental illness and substance abuse are other causes. There are even more reasons why people find themselves homeless.

People can experience temporary or **chronic homelessness**. **Temporary homelessness** is being homeless for less than a year. It is much more common than chronic homelessness, which is being homeless for more than a year. Chronic homelessness can also refer to people who have at least four episodes of homelessness in the past three years.

Being homeless makes it very hard for people to get their basic needs met. Hunger is a constant problem. Injury and illness are threats. Finding food, water, shelter and warmth become the most important things to someone on the streets. Daily life is a struggle to survive. Homelessness affects society, families, teenagers and young children. It is an issue that cannot be ignored.

Life on the streets can be very difficult.

CHAPTER ONE

NOWHERE TO GO

Karen lived in a quiet suburban neighbourhood. It was not a place where homelessness was often seen. Her mother had mental health issues, however, and kicked Karen out one night. It was the first of many nights the 15-year-old found herself without a home.

A woman gives money to a homeless girl in need.

Karen slept on some friends' sofas and even in someone's garden. However, she was not allowed to stay in any one place for too long. She wandered the streets at night and tried to find sheltered places to sleep, such as shop doorways. The doorways stopped the effects of the wind and helped to keep her dry during the long, cold night. It was a terrifying life for a teenager.

BREAKING NEWS

>> In autumn 2014, the number of people in England who were sleeping rough was 2,744. This is a 14 per cent increase from 2013.

Many homeless people use signs to ask for money, food, work or other help.

A COMMON STORY

Thousands of teenagers and children are made homeless every day. Although many have parents with them, there are many who are alone on the streets.

Some teenagers and children might be homeless because they were kicked out of their homes by their parents, just like Karen. People may also become homeless for several other reasons.

London had 742 rough sleepers, which accounted for 27 per cent of the national figure. The number of rough sleepers in London has increased by 37 per cent, compared with an increase of 7 per cent in the rest of England.

A stereotype about homeless people is that they are drug addicts or people who have mental health issues. This is true for many people who have been homeless for long periods of time. It may also be the cause of their homelessness.

For example, of rough sleepers in London, 53 per cent have problems with alcohol and 39 per cent with drugs. In 2011, the charity Crisis found that drug and alcohol abuse accounts for more than one-third of all homeless deaths.

DIFFERENT REASONS

People become homeless for many reasons. Poverty or a financial crisis are two major reasons. A job loss can cause missed rent or **mortgage** payments. Even if a person is working full time, earning the minimum wage, he or she may not be able to afford the rent required to house a family, and may have to apply for housing benefit. If an emergency or the death of a family member occurs, a family can become temporarily homeless.

Domestic violence is one cause of homelessness.

BREAKING NEWS

>> Housing First is a service run by the charity Changing Lives. The service aims to provide support to long-term and recurrently homeless people.

Sometimes, a person's family life is filled with abuse or conflict. Domestic violence can force women and children to leave their homes. Divorce, sexual abuse or neglect can cause homelessness, too. Lesbian, gay, bisexual or transgender (LGBT) teenagers who come out to their parents may not be accepted – many teenagers are thrown out of their homes because of their sexuality.

Those who have served in the armed forces are another growing homeless group. Some soldiers come back from war with physical **disabilities** or mental health issues. As a result, it becomes difficult for them to maintain normal civilian lives. Sometimes, these problems lead to **addiction** or violence and the soldiers may lose their homes as a result.

Some people become homeless due to mental illnesses or physical disabilities.

Recent research carried out by the charity found that its average client has been homeless for 14 years.

Most people experience homelessness for only a short period of time. This is called **transitional homelessness.** A major crisis, such as a natural disaster, a job loss or a medical condition usually causes transitional homelessness. This crisis causes a family or individual to become homeless. In some countries, a lack of affordable housing can be a major cause of homelessness for families with children. Poverty, unemployment, **eviction** and domestic violence are other leading causes.

When floods struck the United Kingdom in 2012, many people were left temporarily homeless.

UNDERCOVER STORY

FINDING HOMES

There are many organizations that work to house the homeless. Changing Lives has successfully housed people who were stuck in a cycle of rough sleeping, **sofa-surfing**, hostels, prison and sometimes hospital. The project supports clients to secure their own **tenancy**. For many, having a home is not just a solution to sleeping rough, but it offers them a chance to start over. The charity found that those clients with a history of substance abuse said that securing a tenancy had helped them to maintain **abstinence**. It also helped them to continue taking their medication.

A PLACE TO STAY

If families or individuals lose their homes, they most likely will spend some time with friends or family, sleeping on sofas or in spare rooms. With this support, they can work and save money to get back into their own homes again. Without friends or family to offer a place to stay, some people have nowhere to go. These temporarily homeless people may sleep in their cars or find a place that offers transitional housing. In 2013/14 in the United Kingdom, 38 per cent of all people sleeping rough were booked into accommodation.

Homeless people who are given some form of accommodation often require temporary housing for only a short period of time. They are then able to support themselves once again.

People who are chronically homeless have very different needs. They need more than just a little time to get back on their feet. To stay in permanent housing, they may need help for the rest of their lives.

A chronically homeless person has been homeless for a long period of time. Most have a serious mental illness, a substance addiction or a physical disability. For example, he or she could be suffering from schizophrenia. This is a brain disorder that causes voices in a person's head and feelings of paranoia. It can be difficult for a person with this disorder to function in daily life. A chronically homeless person may have a severe addiction problem. A physical disability could also prevent someone from holding down a job and paying the bills. These are not problems that can be easily fixed.

Chronically homeless people may never be able to live in permanent housing without support.

BREAKING NEWS

>> According to figures for 2013/14 from the Combined Homelessness and Information Network (CHAIN), of those people sleeping rough in London, around 58 per cent slept rough just once during the

ring

THE HOMELESS CYCLE

The chronically homeless may spend decades going from hospitals to emergency shelters to living on the streets. They may even end up in prisons. They cycle through different programmes and treatments, ending back on the streets once more. These people require permanent housing help and other types of support to end their cycle of homelessness.

A physical disability may prevent a homeless person from getting a job.

year, 70 per cent were new to sleeping rough, but around 11 per cent were considered "returners" – those who were seen sleeping rough before 2012/13, but were not seen during 2012/13.

CHAPTER TWO

HOMELESS TEENAGERS

It can be hard to tell that someone is homeless. For example, Lulu looks just like any other teenage girl – except she became homeless when she was 12. Before that, she took care of her ill mother for four years. Lulu never met her alcoholic father, who never paid child maintenance to her mother. Then, Lulu's mother died from lung cancer in 2003. Lulu was the only one at home when it happened. Her aunt and grandfather also died that year. Suddenly, Lulu was left alone and had to fend for herself.

Being homeless is incredibly stressful for teenagers.

BREAKING NEWS

>> Establishing an accurate count of homeless teenagers is difficult. Most try to stay hidden. In the United Kingdom, 52 per cent of those seeking help

Lulu went to 14 foster homes and seven hostels in the six years after her mother died. They were never places in which she wanted to stay. Lulu ran away from each home. Eventually, she met a boy and moved in with his friend and family into a single, cramped flat. She and her boyfriend paid the family money each week to stay there. It was either there or the shelter. However, Lulu was trying to find a place for herself and her boyfriend. Soon there would be three of them – Lulu was pregnant.

ONE OF MANY

Lulu is just one of many teenagers on the streets. The exact number of homeless youth at any one time is hard to estimate. This is because many teenagers do not use shelters – they are afraid that they will be sent into the foster care system. It is at shelters and other services that homeless counts are made.

Homeless teenagers may not know where to go to find help.

with homelessness are under 25 years of age, and 60 per cent of these young people are not in education, training or employment.

Teenagers on the street are **vulnerable**. The street is a hostile environment for anyone, let alone a teenager. Most teenagers need help to survive. They become easy targets for adult **predators**, who can offer food, money or a bed in which to sleep. However, the results can be sexual, mental and physical abuse. So, why do teenagers leave the safety of a home for the streets? They leave because many do not come from safe homes to begin with.

Family problems are a major cause of teenager homelessness.

BREAKING NEWS

>> In 2014, the Albert Kennedy Trust (AKT) provided 8,000 nights off the streets for young LGBT people with nowhere else to turn.

PROBLEMS AT HOME

Many homeless teenagers leave home because of problems within their families. There may be abuse in their home. This abuse might be domestic violence between parents. A parent or other family member may also sexually or physically abuse a teenager at home. Substance abuse by a parent, or mental illness, may be other causes of abuse.

Many LGBT homeless youths report that family rejection is the cause of their homelessness.

These disorders may result in the neglect of children in the home. A parent's job or home loss may also cause his or her teenager's homelessness.

Parents may reject their LGBT children when they come out. These teenagers may then be forced to leave their homes because of their sexuality. AKT says that LGBT people make up 24 per cent of the homeless youth population in the United Kingdom.

The foster, juvenile justice and mental health systems often fail to support young people. These systems only support teenagers until they turn 18. Then, they are released into the world to care for themselves. Many do not have any family or financial support system. These young people may also lack basic life skills.

Once they leave home, teenagers must quickly learn how to deal with life on the streets. Not having a home makes the most simple things much more difficult. Homeless teenagers must carry everything they need with them at all times. They have no place to store clothes, blankets, toothbrushes or any other personal items they own.

Finding a dry, warm and safe place to sleep is another immediate concern. Teenagers might sleep under bridges, in tents or in abandoned garages or houses. These are not safe places to sleep, however. Some teenagers try to sleep during the day, when it is less likely that they may be attacked. They stay awake at night and walk the streets.

Many teenagers ask strangers for money to buy food.

UNDERCOVER STORY

TEENAGE BEGGARS

Most homeless teenagers cannot work at a job. They may not be old enough or be eligible for different jobs, or keeping a job may become impossible. To get money for food, many homeless young people beg or ask strangers to give them money. It can be humiliating for homeless people to do this, but it is a last resort in order to be able to buy food. In England and Wales there are laws against begging and being a public nuisance, making things even harder.

FINDING FOOD

Food and water are other constant concerns for homeless teenagers. If teenagers have money, they may be able to buy food. However, many do not, and rely on strangers to give them food. These teenagers may also search for unused or leftover food that has been thrown in the rubbish at restaurants.

Some desperate teenagers even steal food from shops.

Homeless young people do not have easy access to bathrooms or showers. This makes it difficult for them to stay clean and wash their clothes. Being unclean is a problem in itself, because it can lead to a number of health issues.

School can be the one place homeless teenagers find stability and many continue to go to school, despite the challenges this entails. However, school has its own difficulties for homeless pupils. Most homeless pupils do not want other pupils to know that they are homeless, so they work hard to hide it from their friends and classmates. If found out, homeless teenagers are at risk of being bullied or teased by their peers.

It is also very difficult for homeless pupils to maintain their studies. They may not have a place to study and do coursework, so they fall behind and do not get the marks needed. They may not have a safe place to sleep, so they come to school exhausted. Without money for public transport, it may also be difficult for these pupils to get to school every day. In addition to all this, the stress of being homeless affects their ability to do schoolwork.

Homeless pupils are so exhausted that they even fall asleep in class.

BREAKING NEWS

>> In November 2014, the charity Shelter said that more than 90,000 children in England, Scotland and Wales were without a permanent home.

SNOWBALL EFFECT

These substantial problems all add up, affecting how well homeless pupils do in school. Over time, being homeless can seriously affect a pupil's achievement. Pupils can develop learning problems and have low numeracy and literacy skills. If these problems are not addressed, these pupils leave school without the skills needed to succeed. They may fail to get jobs and to become independent adults who can support themselves.

Teachers and school counsellors can offer help to homeless teenagers, however. They can tell homeless pupils about available community services. Some schools offer special services for their homeless pupils. They include showering facilities, meals, clean clothes and extended after-school activities.

HITTING THE HEADLINES

ONCE HOMELESS, NOW A CAMBRIDGE GRADUATE

Poppy Noor was born to a cab-driving father and a mother who was diagnosed with severe mental illness when Poppy was eight years old. Her father was in and out of prison and her home life was unstable, dysfunctional and unsafe. At 16 years old, Poppy felt she had no option but to leave. She moved through six different hostels and bed and breakfast accommodation. Despite this, Poppy worked hard during her sixth form and she was given a place at Cambridge University. She graduated and now works for local government.

CHAPTER THREE

SURVIVING HOMELESSNESS

When Tiffany's parents died, she went to live with her auntie and uncle. However, they did not like the fact that Tiffany was a lesbian. She was kicked out of their home when she was just 15.

Tiffany was also being bullied at school because of her sexuality. She dropped out of school and fell into a deep depression. She tried to kill herself, overdosing on painkillers. Tiffany survived the overdose, but living on the streets was incredibly hard. Some nights were spent sleeping on roofs during rainstorms.

Tiffany was on the streets for seven years. She is one of many young people who are kicked out of their homes for being gay.

Activists have taken to London's streets to raise awareness for LGBT youth homelessness.

ENDING LGBT YOUTH HOMELESSNESS

London: 020 7831 6562   Manchester: 0161 228 3308   Website: www.akt.org.uk

BREAKING NEWS

>> Most homeless teenagers do not receive the health care that they need. Many also have multiple health problems. They have poor diets, which leads to malnutrition.

STREET LIFE

Being on the streets is tough. Depression or other mental illnesses are common among homeless young people. They must watch their backs. They worry constantly, wondering where they can find food or sleep each night.

They miss having families and people who care for and love them. They also have to blend in with the homeless population to avoid sexual predators. There are many physical and mental dangers for homeless teenagers.

Drug and alcohol abuse is common among homeless teenagers.

Some teenagers abuse substances and many have emotional or mental issues. Some homeless young people develop chronic health issues because of their lack of medical care. These health issues include asthma, diabetes and epilepsy.

The longer a teenager remains homeless, the more likely it is that homelessness will have serious health effects. It is physically demanding to be homeless. Without shelter, young people are exposed to harsh weather and temperatures. They may get frostbite or have wounds that do not heal fully. Being exposed can weaken people's immune systems. They are likely to become ill more often than housed teenagers, contracting bronchitis, pneumonia or other illnesses. Homeless teenagers are also less likely to seek or receive medical care. They do not want to be returned to their families or be forced into foster care.

Being homeless can cause serious long-term health issues.

HITTING THE HEADLINES

FROM STAR TO HOMELESS ADDICT

Natasha Lyonne first became famous when she played Jessica in the *American Pie* series. She also appeared in the *Slums of Beverly Hills*, *Everyone Says I Love You*, *Blade: Trinity* and *But I'm a Cheerleader*. During her early acting years, Lyonne suffered from substance abuse. In 2001, she was arrested for driving under the influence of alcohol. Then, in 2003, Lyonne was evicted by her landlord. She was homeless and battling addictions. After open-heart surgery and treatment for her drug abuse, Lyonne won the role of Nicky Nichols in the Netflix Original Series, *Orange is the New Black*.

USING DRUGS TO COPE

Teenagers are also exposed to drug use while on the streets. They may have tried or used drugs before they were homeless, or they may start while homeless. Some people use drugs to cope with the stress and **anxiety** that comes with living on the streets. However, the drugs just end up making their problems worse. For some, the drug use turns to addiction. An addiction can make it even harder for teenagers to find permanent housing or a job. Dealing with an addiction usually also requires specialist medical help. Coming off drugs is a difficult process for most people. It is even more difficult for a homeless person, who struggles to meet his or her basic needs every day. An addiction of any form also brings its own set of health issues.

Being homeless can make people feel invisible to society. Many people look past the homeless, as though they cannot see them. Homeless people can start to feel disconnected from society – as if they do not even belong to it anymore. It is important to remember that anyone can become homeless. This is a reality that most people do not want to face, so they choose to ignore it instead. However, feeling invisible and ignored can be emotionally difficult for homeless people and can wear down their self-esteem.

The feelings of alienation from society are why homeless teenagers try to connect with others on the street. It also helps to be part of a group. Then they are less vulnerable to dangerous adults. Homeless young people create street families – friendships with other, more experienced homeless teenagers. The more experienced teach the less experienced how to survive. They protect each other, but the protection usually comes at a price. These families may have abusive and unhealthy types of relationships, involving sex and substance abuse.

UNDERCOVER STORY

HOMELESS HATE CRIMES

A hate crime is an act of violence against a person or group of people based on someone's hatred for that type of person or group. Some people target the homeless for hate crimes. These crimes include beatings, rapes and setting people on fire. Crisis says that, compared with the general public, homeless people are 13 times more likely to have experienced violence and 47 times more likely to be victims of theft. Almost one in 10 homeless people experience a sexual assault each year.

USING SEX TO SURVIVE

Survival sex is one common problem with homeless young people. Many trade sex for food, clothes, money or drugs. Most teenagers do not have money to buy what they need and do not want to go to shelters, so they believe sex is the most valuable thing they can trade. However, this sexual trade exploits vulnerable young people and can have terrible results. Teenagers may contract **sexually transmitted diseases** or find themselves with unwanted pregnancies.

A homeless couple begs for help on a city street. Relationships between homeless teenagers can be based on survival, not love.

Young people may leave home because they are being sexually or physically abused. They escape to the streets, but there they are at risk of even more abuse. According to Crisis, around 8 per cent of homeless people are sexually assaulted. Around 3 per cent of these attacks are by the public and not other homeless people.

Predatory adults look for young people alone on the streets. These adults try to find young people they can lure to come with them to another place. Teenagers on their own are both vulnerable and scared, and the adults may promise them food, clothing or money. They give them attention and may even tell them that they are special or loved. However, the predatory adults are not trying to help these teenagers. They want to sexually or physically abuse them. These predatory adults may be pimps, drug dealers or criminals.

The stress of being homeless can lead to mental illnesses.

BREAKING NEWS

>> According to a research briefing by Crisis published in 2011, homeless people are more than nine times more likely to commit suicide than the general population.

MENTAL HEALTH ISSUES

Many homeless young people also have a mental illness. They develop emotional problems, such as depression and post-traumatic stress disorder (PTSD), as a result of their difficult experiences. They do not know how to deal with their physical or sexual abuse. They have anxiety or high levels of stress, constantly worried about finding food or shelter. They also worry about being assaulted by strangers. Their mental illness may lead them to attempt suicide. Most do not receive medication or therapy to help with their illnesses.

A homeless teenager who is alone is vulnerable to predatory adults.

CHAPTER FOUR

GETTING OFF THE STREETS

Twelve-year-old Carissa ran from a bad situation at home to a worse one on the streets. Her stepfather was abusive, beating up her brothers and trying to abuse her sister. Her mother did not do anything to protect Carissa and her 10 siblings. Carissa felt she had to leave.

Carissa went from homes to young offender institutions but ended up on the streets. She was vulnerable and became a **prostitute**. Her world was filled with violence, rape and homelessness. Carissa was looking for loving attention and sexual predators knew how to exploit her.

The help of an adult is important to teenagers who want to get off the streets.

BREAKING NEWS

>> In the United Kingdom, 25 per cent of young, homeless women have engaged in sex work to fund accommodation or in the hope of getting a bed for the night.

However, at the young offender institution, Carissa also gained the attention of mentors. These mentors saved her from a life of violence and abuse. Counsellors and teachers saw Carissa's great potential. They encouraged her to get an education and set goals for herself. Carissa did – and ended up achieving them all.

Carissa went to law school and then business school. She now speaks out about youth homelessness. She said, "And now with my story, with coming out and seeing the problem the way it is right now, I can do that for people that are voiceless, people that are homeless. Kids that are just invisible, I can stand up and fight for them and it's a wonderful feeling."

HOPE FOR THE FUTURE

There is always hope that a person can escape homelessness. Carissa escaped with the help of mentors. Homeless teenagers can find help in schools and shelters, youth programmes and religious organizations. Sometimes, all it takes is just one person to make a huge difference in a homeless teenager's life.

A homeless teenager faces many obstacles to education and employment.

Organizations provide different services to help homeless teenagers. Some places have van or street outreach programmes in which members of the organization go to the streets to find homeless young people. They might give the teenagers a sandwich or tell them where they can get free, clean clothes. They will also let homeless young people know what services their organization provides.

Homeless shelters provide short-term services to homeless teenagers. The young people can get a bed for a night and free meals. They can take a shower and maybe get some new clothes. Teenagers can also talk with counsellors. These counsellors try to understand why these young people are homeless, offering advice or information to help them. The counsellors can also help the teenagers to reconnect with their families.

CONTINUING HELP

Transitional housing helps homeless teenagers for longer periods of time. Homeless young people can continue with counselling and get help with their education. They can also learn life skills and receive medical attention and care. Teenagers can also get help with finding a job. The goal of transitional housing is to help homeless young people to live independently. There are different organizations that focus on specific needs, such as teenagers who have alcohol or drug addictions, or single teenage mothers.

Permanent supportive housing is also available for homeless young people. It is generally for the chronically homeless who need support for their entire lives. They pay a small percentage of their rent. Government **grants** pay the rest of their rent.

Opposite: Many homeless shelters provide holiday and other meals for people in need of food.

BREAKING NEWS

>> There are around 400,000 hidden homeless in the United Kingdom, living out of sight in hostels, bed and breakfasts, sofa-surfing or squatting.

Some programmes help homeless people to develop specific skills, such as art or job skills. The Scottish sandwich chain Social Bite is more than just a sandwich shop. The company employs homeless people to help get them off the streets – one in four of the company's team is formerly homeless. Social Bite also feeds the local homeless community through their "Suspended Coffee and Food" initiative. Programmes such as this one give homeless people job training and they also boost their self-esteem.

CONNECTING THROUGH ART

Another great way to connect with homeless people is through art.

Art, such as legal graffiti, is a great way to connect with troubled teenagers.

Get Creative: Arts for All works across England to give homeless people access to the arts. This may be through participation in creative activities within a hostel or day centre, or through engaging in arts and cultural activities and events in the community. The programme helps people to develop their artistic skills and to develop relationships with mentors. Art can be an amazing tool through which to express feelings. This is something that may be difficult for homeless teenagers to do.

Different programmes have a lot to offer to homeless people, in particular homeless teenagers. However, many teenagers avoid programmes in an attempt to stay hidden, afraid they will be forced to go into foster care or back to abusive homes. By connecting with young people via their passions, such as art or music, programmes can more easily reach vulnerable young people and deliver their services to them.

UNDERCOVER STORY
INOCENTE IZUCAR

The documentary *Inocente* won an Oscar in 2013. It tells the story of Inocente Izucar, a homeless teenage artist in San Diego, United States. She was in an art programme called ARTS: A Reason to Survive. The programme was a refuge for Inocente from her problems at school and with her mother. The documentary leads up to Inocente's first art show. The film changed her life, too. In 2012, Inocente was supporting herself by selling her paintings. Art was able to get Inocente off the streets and to raise awareness of the problem of teenage homelessness.

CHAPTER FIVE

SOCIETY AND HOMELESSNESS

The problem of homelessness is growing and some cities are responding with law enforcement. In these cases, laws that target the activities of homeless people are brought into force. In the United Kingdom, the Vagrancy Act of 1824 made it an offence to sleep rough or beg. Anyone found to be homeless or trying to beg money can be arrested. Some cities employ extra officers to enforce the laws. They hope that the laws will drive homeless people from their cities. Some states in the United States also have similar laws. For example, in Sarasota, Florida and Lawrence, Kansas, it is illegal to sleep outdoors and panhandle, or beg, for money.

This homeless man is sleeping in a public park. If he is reported, he could be arrested or made to leave.

BREAKING NEWS

>> The Anti-Social Behaviour, Crime and Policing Act 2014, took effect from October that year. The law defines anti-social behaviour as, "conduct capable of causing nuisance or annoyance to a person in relation to that person's occupation

ENDING UP IN PRISON

The results of these laws are that homeless people end up in the criminal justice system. They may spend time in prison and have criminal records. This can be especially damaging to young people who are placed in prisons with tough criminals.

Once arrested, teenagers may enter the justice system and gain criminal records.

Some people believe that arresting homeless people is not a solution to the problem at all. If anything, it just makes the problem worse. A criminal record makes it even harder for a homeless person to find employment or housing. The costs of the justice system are also higher than the costs of providing supportive housing. Is it right to arrest someone for not having a home? Many people believe it is not. They believe it violates a homeless person's rights.

of residential premises or conduct capable of causing housing-related nuisance or annoyance to any person." This could be interpreted to include begging and it means police can fine and arrest those breaking this law. In 2013, a total of 700 people were arrested for begging in London. With this law in place, this number is set to rise.

Communities recognize that homelessness is a growing problem. That is why there are many services available for the homeless. These services are offered at the local, county and national levels.

Many churches and charities run programmes to help the homeless. Individuals in communities donate to these charities. They might give clothing, money or food. Then the charities distribute the goods to those in need. Some services help a person who is at risk of becoming homeless. They provide small grants to help with mortgage or rent payments. These local charities and organizations also run shelters, housing facilities, medical clinics and food banks. Shelter and Centrepoint are two organizations that provide help for the homeless.

Different charities feed, house and counsel homeless teenagers and adults.

HOUSING BENEFITS

The government has a housing benefits system to help those who can no longer pay their rent or service charges. The benefit does not cover mortgages, ensuring that help is given to those who have low income or are on unemployment benefits. To qualify for housing benefits, a person's savings must be lower than £16,000.

In 2014, there were 27,970 applications for assistance between 1 July and 30 September: of these applications, 50 per cent were accepted but of the other 50 per cent, 18 per cent were found to be homeless but not in priority need, 8 per cent were found to be intentionally homeless and in priority need. The remaining 24 per cent were found not to be homeless.

Several programmes provide funding to get people off the streets and into housing.

HITTING THE HEADLINES
HOMES FOR ABUSED WOMEN

In the United Kingdom, there are refuges for abused women and their families. The refuges are at secret locations so that women will be safe there. To get a place in a women's shelter, a woman must call the National Domestic Violence helpline, and a counsellor will help her to find a suitable place to stay.

Prevention is one key factor to ending homelessness. Prevention for adults can mean receiving money to help with rent or mortgage payments during difficult times. A family can become homeless after missing just one of these payments. With small grants, families gain time to find work or come up with a plan to stop them losing their homes.

Counselling can help to prevent a teenager from becoming homeless.

For teenagers, prevention may come in the form of intervention from a counsellor or a social worker. If families are fighting, therapy may help to solve their problems. Or in cases of neglect or abuse, a social worker can place a teenager or child in a safer situation. Parents can also be educated about being more involved with their children's lives. If substance abuse or mental illness is affecting their children,

UNDERCOVER STORY

NATIONAL SLEEP OUT

Every November, homeless charity Centrepoint and its partners organize a national sleep out to raise awareness of youth homelessness. Around the country, participants brave the cold winter weather with nothing but their sleeping bag and a cardboard mat. In 2014, more than 1,000 people "slept rough" for Centrepoint in London and a further 2,000 slept out around the country. Together, they raised more than £420,000.

they may be better able to notice the signs and offer help. Offering help could prevent their children from running away from home and becoming homeless.

THE POWER OF MEDIA

The media are also a powerful tool for educating the public about homelessness. Scottish charity leaders and well-known faces from the worlds of politics and entertainment have joined forces in a campaign to reduce youth homelessness. The campaign called "Stop. Talk. Listen." asks people to upload a selfie to a social media wall – revealing "what's been the biggest cause of arguments at home?"

This is just one of many media campaigns aimed at educating the public about homelessness. Just knowing about the problem can help to prevent and solve the issue.

Homelessness can have some lasting effects on society. Without help, homeless teenagers can grow up to be troubled adults. Troubled adults may not reach their full potential and may not be able to contribute to their communities.

Since homelessness usually interrupts education, a homeless young person may educationally lag behind his or her peers.

This has a ripple effect that follows the teenager into adulthood. Without support, a homeless young person may not complete a secondary school education. University then becomes difficult or even impossible. Without education or job training, homeless teenagers can become unemployable adults or people who may only be able to find jobs that do not pay a living wage. These adults then add to the unemployment rate.

HITTING THE HEADLINES

VACANT HOMES FOR THE HOMELESS?

Due to hard economic times, many cities are filled with vacant homes. Some city authorities are considering housing the homeless in those vacant homes. Some believe this would be the ideal solution to the problem of homelessness, especially since there are so many vacant homes. According to figures collated by the *Guardian* newspaper from across the EU, more than 11 million homes lie empty across Europe – enough to house all of the continent's homeless twice over.

THE CRIMINAL CYCLE

If young people enter the justice system because they are homeless, it can be more damaging than helpful. Many kinds of criminal are in the justice system. Homeless young people are then exposed to violence and different kinds of criminal activity. In prison, homeless teenagers can be treated like dangerous criminals. Studies have shown that it also costs more to keep homeless teenagers in prison than it costs to provide them with housing. Another problem facing those who have served a prison sentence is that once they leave the justice system, it may be even harder to move back towards an independent life in society. There are few job opportunities for homeless teenagers and even fewer for those who are homeless and who have served time. The offenders may find themselves in prison again.

Some cities are considering repairing vacant homes to house the homeless.

HOMELESSNESS –
THE WHOLE STORY

Being homeless is not something anyone wishes for, but it is a situation that many people face every year. Homelessness affects all kinds of people, from the man who loses his job to the teenager trying to escape abuse at home. People become homeless for many different reasons. Sometimes, substance abuse is involved or a parent cannot find a job that pays enough to rent a home for his or her family. Sometimes, a parent cannot accept a teenager's sexuality and forces the young person to leave his or her home. Whatever the reason, the reality of life on the streets is harsh.

With help, homeless teenagers can make it off the streets to become independent and successful adults.

UNDERCOVER STORY
MIMI'S JOURNEY

Mimi never had a supportive family. She was excluded from meals and family activities. At home, she suffered constant abuse, and she believed that she would not survive on her own. When Mimi was 23, she fled her family home. She spent 18 months in a women's refuge and was moved to St Mungo's North London Women's Hostel. She took courses at their Recovery College in IT and others, to give her skills to find a job and prepare her for her own home. She also took courses around confidence, self-esteem and positive relationships. Today, she is a volunteer at St Mungo's, helping others.

PROBLEMS ON THE STREET

Homeless teenagers face many dangers on the street. They are exposed to adult predators and drug and alcohol abuse. They have to find ways to meet their basic needs of food, water and shelter. They may resort to stealing, begging or even survival sex to get by. They must also try to stay in school, do homework and study while being homeless. The stress and fear can lead to mental illnesses. Homelessness can also lead to many health problems, including malnutrition and asthma.

There are services available to help homeless teenagers. Getting those services to the teenagers can be challenging, however. Many want to remain hidden from the system to avoid being sent home or placed into foster care. With help, homeless teenagers can find a path off the streets and they can look forwards to finding a bright and independent future.

GLOSSARY

abstinence avoiding completely

addiction condition in which the body and mind crave and depend on particular substances

anxiety feelings of worry or fear

chronic homelessness being homeless for more than a year or having at least four episodes of homelessness in the past three years

disability physical condition that limits the way a person moves or feels things

domestic violence violence in the home or between family members

eviction removed or told to leave

foster care care for a child by an adult or adults, who are not the child's legal parents, in the adults' home

grant money provided by a local authority, government or public fund

mortgage loan given by a bank to buy a house or other building

predator person who wants to exploit others

prevention stopping something from happening

prostitute person who has sex with someone in exchange for money

rough sleeper person who sleeps on the streets

sexually transmitted disease disease that is spread through sexual contact

sofa-surfing staying for a day or two on a different friend's sofa

squatting living in someone else's empty home illegally

survival sex trading sex for food, clothing, shelter or other things a person needs to survive

temporary homelessness being homeless for less than a year

tenancy paying rent to live in someone else's property

transitional homelessness being homeless for only a short period of time

vulnerable being in a weak position

FIND OUT MORE

BOOKS

Homelessness in the UK (Issues), Cara Acred (Independence Educational Publishers, 2014)

Homelessness (Talk About), Kaye Stearman (Wayland, 2013)

No Fixed Abode, Charlie Carroll (Summersdale, 2013)

Real Stories from Street Children Across the World, Anthony Robinson (Frances Lincoln Children's Books, 2014)

ORGANIZATIONS

Centrepoint
Tel: 0845 466 3400
Address: Central House,
25 Camperdown Street,
London, E1 8DZ
Centrepoint is a charity that aims to help young, homeless people to get their lives back on track. It offers support to more than 8,000 people.

Shelter
Helpline: 0808 800 4444
Website: **england.shelter.org.uk**
Shelter is a charity that offers free, expert housing advice to anyone.

Crisis
Crisis is the national charity for single homeless people.
Website: **www.crisis.org.uk**

St Mungo's
St Mungo's helps people to rebuild their lives and deals with the issues that cause homelessness.
Website:
www.mungosbroadway.org.uk

INDEX